Searchlight BOOKS™

Spy Secrets

Secret Spy Gear

Christy Peterson

Lerner Publications ◆ Minneapolis

Lerner Publications Company
An imprint of Lerner Publishing Group, Inc.
241 First Avenue North
Minneapolis, MN 55401 USA

For reading levels and more information, look up this title at www.lernerbooks.com.

Main body text set in Adrianna Regular.
Typeface provided by Chank.

Editor: Brianna Kaiser **Designer:** Mary Ross **Photo Editor:** Brianna Kaiser

Library of Congress Cataloging-in-Publication Data

Names: Peterson, Christy, author.
Title: Secret spy gear / Christy Peterson.
Description: Minneapolis : Lerner Publications, [2021] | Series: Searchlight books. Spy
    secrets | Includes bibliographical references and index. | Audience: Ages 8–11 |
    Audience: Grades 2–3 | Summary: "Spies have to be innovative to not get caught
    during missions. Readers will learn about wartime spies and the disguises and
    gadgets they used to gain intel"— Provided by publisher.
Identifiers: LCCN 2020009437 (print) | LCCN 2020009438 (ebook) |
    ISBN 9781728404257 (library binding) | ISBN 9781728418698 (ebook)
Subjects: LCSH: Intelligence service—Technological innovations—Juvenile literature. |
    Intelligence service—Methodology—Juvenile literature.
Classification: LCC JF1525.I6 P4793 2021 (print) | LCC JF1525.I6 (ebook) | DDC
    327.12028/4—dc23

LC record available at https://lccn.loc.gov/2020009437
LC ebook record available at https://lccn.loc.gov/2020009438

Manufactured in the United States of America
1-48483-48997-8/18/2020

Table of Contents

Chapter 1

A DANGEROUS MISSION

On a dark night in 1940s France, a parachute jumper floated to the ground. She quickly stripped off a green-and-tan jumpsuit. She pulled a small shovel from its pockets and dug a hole in the ground with the shovel. Then she buried the jumpsuit and the parachute to erase all traces of her jump.

Many spies were used during World War II (1939–1945).

The jumper was a secret agent. Britain sent thousands of agents into enemy territory during World War II. The agents spied on enemy soldiers. They destroyed equipment and vehicles. And they sent important information back to headquarters. Special gear helped them complete their missions.

That's a Fact!

In the James Bond books and movies, a character named Q supplies superspy Bond with cool gear. Q was based on the real-life inventor Charles Fraser-Smith. He worked for a British spy agency during World War II. He used everyday objects to hide useful tools. Hairbrushes hid maps in their handles. Fountain pens hid compasses. The gadgets he invented were called Q gadgets.

English novelist Ian Fleming is best known for his character James Bond.

The Importance of Spying

Spies gather intelligence, or secret information. Countries use spies in wartime to learn what their enemies might be planning. Secret agents also carry out sabotage missions to help their side defeat the enemy. During peacetime, spy agencies continue to gather information. Their work keeps people safe.

Spies are always gathering information.

Spies use many types of gear during their missions. Some agents work to steal information. They might carry a hidden camera to photograph secret papers. Other agents listen in on private conversations. They carry tools that allow them to eavesdrop. Agents also might carry radios for sending messages.

Agents can use special devices to listen in on private conversations.

Spies use gear to sneak into places.

    Gear might help spies sneak into places they are not supposed to be. A spy might carry a disguise or tools to pick a lock. Objects with secret compartments allow spies to stash messages. A tube of shaving cream or a bottle cork might hide secret codes. Sometimes gear helps a spy escape a sticky situation.

Chapter 2

WORKING UNDERCOVER

At a busy café, two strangers meet. One is a handler. Her job is to hire and manage secret agents. The other person is unhappy with the government. The handler hopes that she can convince this person to spy for her country. Just as they are about to sit down, the handler's neighbor walks by. Will she be discovered?

Spies have covers so they can be unrecognized and blend in when out in public.

Luckily, the handler has changed her appearance. Clever makeup and a gray wig make her appear older. A brace on her leg forces her to limp. The neighbor doesn't recognize her. The special gear disguises her for a short time. But sometimes spies need to pretend to be someone else for much longer. This secret identity is called a cover.

Meet a Spy!

In 1941, the United States wanted to learn about Japan's wartime plans. Clarence Yamagata, a Japanese American man, was sent to the Philippines. He spoke Japanese and could blend in with Japanese people living there. He collected secret information for the US by listening to Japanese radio communications. He also taught other Americans to understand the Japanese language. After the war, he was awarded the Legion of Merit for his service.

Clarence Yamagata

Agents may use fake passports as part of their cover.

A spy's secret identity needs to be convincing. Spy agencies give agents fake passports and other paperwork. The agent has to memorize details about the new identity. The agent has to act perfectly as that person. That way, no one will suspect the person is secretly someone else. Together, the spy's paperwork and acting are called a legend.

Tools of the Trade

Spies working undercover need to hide their gear. Tools such as maps and secret codes could break their cover. Everyday objects with secret hiding spaces can be useful. In the twentieth century, one spy in Germany hid her gear in a clothes iron with a secret compartment. Another hid a camera inside a lighter.

SPY TOOLS CAN BE HIDDEN INSIDE EVERYDAY OBJECTS LIKE AN IRON.

Lock-picking kits can help spies sneak into places.

Spies sometimes need to get into places without having permission. Spies might talk their way into secret areas. Or they might steal a key, make a copy, and return it before anyone notices. Sometimes spies receive special training and a lock-picking kit. Whatever the method, agents always have to be sneaky. If someone catches them, their mission will fail.

Chapter 3

GATHERING INTELLIGENCE

Once agents gain access to secrets, they need to record the information. They use special equipment to do this. Spy agencies in the twentieth century used cameras that could be easily disguised. Cameras might look like a pair of glasses or a book. They might be hidden in a watch or a button. Microdot cameras took photos so small that they had to be viewed with a magnifier.

Spies can also gather information using tiny listening devices called bugs. Bugs can be hidden inside walls or objects. One spy agency stole shoes ordered by an American diplomat. The agency hid bugs in the heels of the shoes. Then the shoes were carefully repackaged and sent to the diplomat. Another agency developed a bug that could be slipped into the spine of a book.

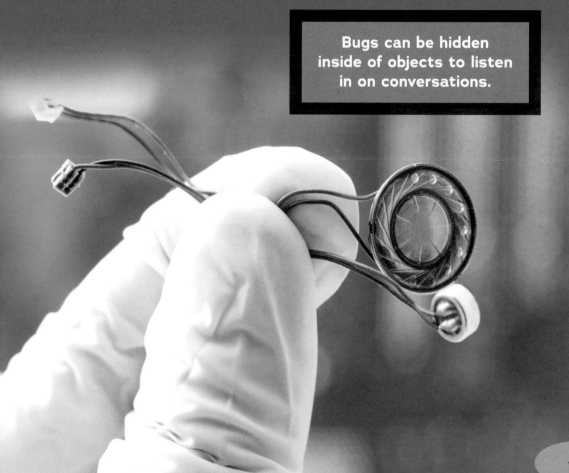

Bugs can be hidden inside of objects to listen in on conversations.

Electronic Eyes and Ears

Sometimes spy agencies use teams of people to gather information. Some team members learn to follow a target without being noticed. They carry several outfits so they can blend in wherever they go. Sweats help them go unnoticed at the gym. Suits make them look natural in an office. Props such as sports equipment or briefcases help complete their looks.

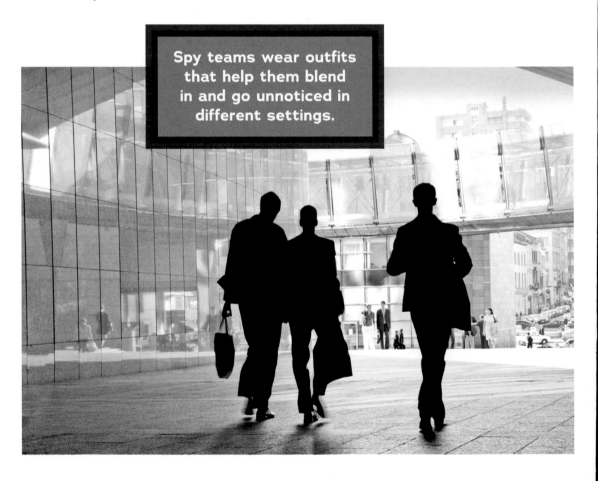

Spy teams wear outfits that help them blend in and go unnoticed in different settings.

Agents use technology to gain information about and to follow their targets.

Other team members use technology to track a target. Agents can track someone using the person's cell phone signal. They use a device that acts like a cell phone tower. They can also tap into networks of security cameras. They use the cameras to follow a person or vehicle. Computer programs help them recognize a person's face.

Keystroke recorders track
what a person types.

Some agents gain access to a target's computer. To break into another computer, an agent might send a program called a keystroke recorder. This program tracks every key typed on a keyboard. By tracking what a person types, an agent can learn passwords. This allows the agent to access their target's computer from miles away.

Spy agencies use drones and satellites. The drones don't spy on one person. Instead, they give a view of a large area. Drones fitted with cameras can look over a whole battlefield. Spy satellites in space can look over a whole city or zoom in on something as small as a Frisbee.

Drones can be used to spy on large areas.

Meet a Spy!

Virginia Hall worked as a secret agent in France during World War II. On one mission, she pretended to be a reporter for the *New York Post*. Late in the war, she organized and trained three groups of resistance fighters. On D-Day, her troops destroyed bridges, derailed trains, and cut phone lines. This helped the Allies force the Germans out of France.

Virginia Hall received the Distinguished Service Cross for her work in France.

Chapter 4

PASSING MESSAGES

On May 20, 1985, the Federal Bureau of Investigation (FBI) watched a car drive down a lonely street. A man jumped out of the car and dropped an empty soda can next to a utility pole. Later, near another utility pole, he hid a trash bag. After he left, the FBI agents investigated. The trash bag contained hundreds of secret military documents. The man who left them, John Walker, was arrested for spying.

UNLIKELY OBJECTS SUCH AS TOILET PAPER HOLDERS CAN SERVE AS HIDING SPOTS FOR SECRET DOCUMENTS.

Walker had placed secret documents in a dead drop. A dead drop is a place where agents leave items for their handlers to pick up. Sometimes a dead drop is a gadget such as a fake rock. One agency made a dead drop out of a toilet paper holder. Other times, a dead drop is an unlikely place such as a trash can.

Passing information can be the most dangerous part of a spy's job. If an agent and handler meet in person, people watching them might get suspicious. A dead drop is one way to avoid detection. But it doesn't always work. In Walker's case, the FBI was already on to him. The bag of documents was the proof they needed to arrest him.

John Walker (*front left*) was arrested for spying.

That's a Fact!

Spy agencies use many creative devices as dead drops. They even used dead rats! One agency removed a rat's organs. This made a space just big enough for messages, money, or film. They attached Velcro so the rat could be opened and closed. Then the rat would be tossed out of a car window at a chosen location. And how did they keep animals from eating the rats? They smeared the rats with hot sauce.

One spy agency used dead rats as dead drops.

Secret Words, Secret Meanings

Agents often use codes and ciphers to pass written and computer messages. In a code, a word or a group of numbers replaces another word. The sender and receiver each have a codebook, or a list of the codes and their meanings. A cipher uses a set of rules to change a letter or number into another letter or number. As long as both parties have the rules, no codebook is needed.

SPIES USE CODES AND CIPHERS TO PASS MESSAGES TO ONE ANOTHER.

Programmers develop ciphers, and codebreakers try to unscramble a cipher's message.

Agencies hire programmers to develop unbreakable ciphers. But their enemies have codebreakers working to unscramble secret communications. Both sides race to develop gear and techniques to outsmart the other side. And spy agencies work hard to give their agents the best tools for the job. With their supercool spy gear, spies can stay safe and uncover valuable secrets.

I Spy!

Need a way to pass a secret message?
A ballpoint pen has the answer. Write a code or
a message on a piece of paper about 3 inches
(7.6 cm) wide and 2 inches (5.1 cm) tall. Then
remove the writing tip of the pen and pull out the
ink tube. Carefully wrap the message around the
ink tube. Then put the ink tube back inside and
reattach the tip of the pen. Don't use a clear pen,
or the secret message will be revealed!

Glossary

bug: a device to secretly listen in on conversations

cipher: a set of rules for changing a letter or number into another character to hide the original letter or number

code: a set of words or phrases that stands for other words or phrases used to communicate in secret

cover: a secret identity

dead drop: a secret place where agents and handlers exchange items

drone: a flying vehicle operated by a remote control

handler: a person who hires and manages spies

intelligence: secret information collected by spies

legend: details about a person's life that help make a cover convincing

spy: a person who steals secret information and passes it along to a spy agency

spy agency: an organization that collects and analyses secret information

Learn More

Central Intelligence Agency: Spy Kids
https://www.cia.gov/kids-page/

International Spy Museum: "Language of Espionage"
https://www.spymuseum.org/education-programs/spy-resources
/language-of-espionage/

Noble, Michael. *The Secret Life of Spies*. London: Wide Eyed Editions, 2020.

Peterson, Christy. *Secret Spy Codes and Messages*. Minneapolis: Lerner Publications, 2021.

Roman, Carole P. *Spies, Code Breakers, and Secret Agents: A World War II Book for Kids*. Emeryville, CA: Rockridge, 2020.

Wonderopolis: "Do Spies Really Use Gadgets?"
https://www.wonderopolis.org/wonder/do-spies-really-use-gadgets

Index

Photo Acknowledgments

Image credits: Sergey Kamshylin/Shutterstock.com, p. 5; McKeown/Express/Getty Images, p. 6; Gorodenkoff/Shutterstock.com, p. 7; Ric011/Shutterstock.com, p. 8; Fractal Pictures/Shutterstock.com, p. 9; djile/Shutterstock.com, p. 11; NSA, p. 12; karenfoleyphotography/Shutterstock.com, p. 13; Carlos Yudica/Shutterstock.com, p. 14; aquatarkus/Shutterstock.com, p. 15; Andrey Burmakin/Shutterstock.com, p. 17; Artens/Shutterstock.com, p. 18; Jacob Lund/Shutterstock.com, p. 19; welcomia/Shutterstock.com, p. 20; Dmitry Kalinovsky/Shutterstock.com, p. 21; Cefaro/wikimdeia commons, p. 22; CapturePB/Shutterstock.com, p. 24; Bettmann/Getty Images, p. 25; Gallinago_media/Shutterstock.com, p. 26; Victor Moussa/Shutterstock.com, p. 27; RossHelen/Shutterstock.com, p. 28; Vladvm/Shutterstock.com, p. 29.

Cover: b.asia/Shutterstock.com.